Writers Inspiring Writers

INSIGHT FROM FAMOUS WRITERS
TO KEEP YOU WRITING 365 DAYS A YEAR

Writers Inspiring Writers

MATTHEW KELLY

BLUE SPARROW
North Palm Beach, Florida

blue sparrow

Copyright © 2019
Kakadu, LLC
Published by BLUE SPARROW

All rights reserved.
No part of this book may be used or reproduced in any
manner whatsoever without permission except in the case
of brief quotations in critical articles or reviews.

The quotes in this book have been drawn from dozens
of sources. They are assumed to be accurate as quoted in
their previously published forms. Although every effort
has been made to verify the quotes and sources, the
Publisher cannot guarantee their perfect accuracy.

Design & Illustration by Ashley Wirfel

ISBN: 978-1-63582-147-5 (hardcover)
ISBN: 978-1-63582-146-8 (e-Book)

10 9 8 7 6 5 4 3 2 1

Printed in the United States of America

FIRST EDITION

Table of Contents

INTRODUCTION
1

JANUARY
5

FEBRUARY
37

MARCH
67

APRIL
99

MAY
131

JUNE
163

JULY
195

AUGUST
227

SEPTEMBER
259

OCTOBER
291

NOVEMBER
323

DECEMBER
355

Introduction

A FEW WEEKS AGO, I was talking to a friend of mine about the busyness of my life. The conversation reached its climax when I said out of frustration, "I really want to be a writer."

My friend looked at me and asked, "How many books have you written?" "About thirty," I replied. "How many bestsellers have you had?" he continued. "A few." "How many millions of copies have your books sold collectively?" I stopped answering, he was on a roll. "And didn't I read somewhere that your books have been published in more than twenty-five languages?"

"So let me summarize," he said, "You have published so many books you don't even know exactly how many, your books have sold more than forty-million copies collectively, been published in twenty-five languages, and you have had more than a dozen bestsellers. Now, I just want you to say what you said a minute ago. Say it out loud and try to hear how ridiculous it sounds."

"I really want to be a writer," I muttered reluctantly.

What I was trying to say was that I yearn for the life of a writer, someone whom I imagine has nothing else to do but write each day. I cannot help but wonder what I might write if I had more time to focus on my craft. The assumption of course is that if I had more time, my writing would improve. Perhaps all that time would allow me to spoil it, like cooking good food for too long. We have all read work that has been massaged and edited too much. It starts to taste and feel artificial rather than real.

So, even after a quarter of a century writing, I don't really feel like a writer. I wake each morning hoping I will write and write well. There are great days, days of great despair, but mostly average days. Moving those average days to great days can make all the difference. It is on those days that I turn to the great writers of any age in search of even an ounce of insight or inspiration to get me started or give me a lift. On these pages you will find what I have found.

The hardest thing about writing is getting started. These brief passages will serve you as they have served me. They will inspire you to write, but most of all, they will stir your spirit and get you started. For it is the beginning that is excruciating. They are purposefully short. Once you have momentum you can write your heart out—and you need to, because that's what great writers do: they write their hearts out. It is the getting started that has so many writers around the world stuck right now, at this very moment, as you read these words.

It is my hope that each short passage is enough to launch you into the day. Now write. Just write. Every day. And then let's see what happens…

January

JANUARY 1

"Nobody ever became a writer merely by wanting to be one."

F. Scott Fitzgerald

JANUARY 2

"Find out the reason that commands you to write; see whether it has spread its roots into the very depth of your heart; confess to yourself you would have to die if you were forbidden to write."

Rainer Maria Rilke

JANUARY 3

"A writer who waits for ideal conditions under which to work will die without putting a word on paper."

E. B. White

JANUARY 4

"A small daily task, if it be really daily, will beat the labors of a spasmodic Hercules."

Anthony Trollope

JANUARY 5

"Perfectionism is the voice of the oppressor, the enemy of the people. It will keep you cramped and insane your whole life, and it is the main obstacle between you and a first draft. I think perfectionism is based on the obsessive belief that if you run carefully enough, hitting each stepping-stone just right, you won't have to die. The truth is that you will die anyway and that a lot of people who aren't even looking at their feet are going to do a whole lot better than you, and have a lot more fun while they're doing it."

Anne Lamott

JANUARY 6

"When I am working on a book or story I write every morning as soon after first light as possible. There is no one to disturb you and it is cool or cold and you come to your work and warm as you write."

Ernest Hemingway

JANUARY 7

"I can write anywhere. I write in airports. I write on airplanes. I've written in the back seats of taxis. I write in hotel rooms. I love hotel rooms. I just write wherever I am whenever I need to write."

Garrison Keillor

JANUARY 8

"For the last three or four novels, I've copied John Steinbeck's activity from *East of Eden*, and I've begun every day by writing in a journal, sometimes about the writing I'm doing, sometimes about what's on my mind at the moment. So for each novel I now write, I create a new journal entry, but before I do that, I read a day in the last Journal of a Novel for the previous novel. This allows me to see that, whatever I might be experiencing at the moment, I have experienced it and survived it before."

Elizabeth George

JANUARY 9

"What I try to do is write. I may write for two weeks 'the cat sat on the mat, that is that, not a rat.' And it might be just the most boring and awful stuff. But I try. When I'm writing, I write. And then it's as if the muse is convinced that I'm serious and says, 'Okay. Okay. I'll come.'"

Maya Angelou

JANUARY 10

"You put your time where your priority is."

Sebastian Faulks

JANUARY 11

"Keep a notebook handy or carry it with you so that you can jot down thoughts that occur to you at odd moments."

Damon Knight

JANUARY 12

"If you're just starting out as a writer, you could do worse than strip your television's electric plug-wire, wrap a spike around it, and then stick it back into the wall. See what blows, and how far. Just an idea."

Stephen King

JANUARY 13

"Put it [your writing] aside for a few days, or longer, do other things, try not to think about it. Then sit down and read it (printouts are best I find, but that's just me) as if you've never seen it before. Start at the beginning. Scribble on the manuscript as you go if you see anything you want to change. And often, when you get to the end you'll be both enthusiastic about it and know what the next few words are. And you do it all one word at a time."

Neil Gaiman

JANUARY 14

"If you get stuck, get away from your desk. Take a walk, take a bath, go to sleep, make a pie, draw, listen to music, meditate, exercise; whatever you do, don't just stick there scowling at the problem. But don't make telephone calls or go to a party; if you do, other people's words will pour in where your lost words should be. Open a gap for them, create a space. Be patient."

Hilary Mantel

JANUARY 15

"I am struck by how, except when you're young, you really need to prioritize in life, figuring out in what order you should divide up your time and energy. If you don't get that sort of system set by a certain age, you'll lack focus and your life will be out of balance."

Haruki Murakami

JANUARY 16

"The best time for planning a book is while you're doing the dishes."

Agatha Christie

JANUARY 17

"I write only about two hours every day because that's all the energy I have. But I don't let anything interfere with those two hours, at the same time and the same place."

Flannery O'Connor

JANUARY 18

"I write while my son is at school. At about 7:45 A.M., I walk him there, with the dogs, then walk them for another forty minutes or so, go home and chain myself to the desk a little before 9 A.M., and try not to be distracted until I hear my son plunge through the front door at about 3 P.M."

Geraldine Brooks

JANUARY 19

"I like to get ten pages a day, which amounts to 2,000 words . . . On some days those ten pages come easily; I'm up and out and doing errands by eleven-thirty in the morning . . . More frequently, as I grow older, I find myself eating lunch at my desk and finishing the day's work around one-thirty in the afternoon. Sometimes, when the words come hard, I'm still fiddling around at teatime. Either way is fine with me, but only under dire circumstances do I allow myself to shut down before I get my 2,000 words."

Stephen King

JANUARY 20

"It had at this time become my custom—and it still is my custom, though of late I have become a little lenient to myself—to write with my watch before me, and to require from myself 250 words every quarter of an hour. I have found that the 250 words have been forthcoming as regularly as my watch went . . . This division of time allowed me to produce over ten pages of an ordinary novel volume a day, and if kept up through ten months, would have given as its results three novels of three volumes each in the year."

Anthony Trollope

JANUARY 21

"Let the writer take up surgery or bricklaying if he is interested in technique. There is no mechanical way to get the writing done, no shortcut. The young writer would be a fool to follow a theory. Teach yourself by your own mistakes; people learn only by error. The good artist believes that nobody is good enough to give him advice. He has supreme vanity. No matter how much he admires the old writer, he wants to beat him."

William Faulkner

JANUARY 22

"Advice to young writers who want to get ahead without any annoying delays: don't write about Man, write about a man."

E. B. White

JANUARY 23

"The only way you can write the truth is to assume that what you set down will never be read. Not by any other person, and not even by yourself at some later date. Otherwise you begin excusing yourself. You must see the writing as emerging like a long scroll of ink from the index finger of your right hand; you must see your left hand erasing it."

Margaret Atwood

JANUARY 24

"I have a glass of water or a cup of tea. There's a certain time I sit down, from 8:00 to 8:30, somewhere within that half hour every morning. I have my vitamin pill and my music, sit in the same seat, and the papers are all arranged in the same places. The cumulative purpose of doing these things the same way every day seems to be a way of saying to the mind, you're going to be dreaming soon."

Stephen King

JANUARY 25

"If you're only going to write when you're inspired, you may be a fairly decent poet, but you will never be a novelist—because you're going to have to make your word count today, and those words aren't going to wait for you, whether you're inspired or not. So, you have to write when you're not "inspired." . . .And the weird thing is that six months later, or a year later, you're going to look back and you're not going to remember which scenes you wrote when you were inspired and which scenes you wrote because they had to be written."

Neil Gaiman

JANUARY 26

"The best way is always to stop when you are going good and when you know what will happen next. If you do that every day . . .you will never be stuck. Always stop while you are going good and don't think about it or worry about it until you start to write the next day. That way your subconscious will work on it all the time. But if you think about it consciously or worry about it you will kill it and your brain will be tired before you start."

Ernest Hemingway

JANUARY 27

"It starts by forgetting about perfect. We don't have time for perfect. In any event, perfection is unachievable: It's a myth and a trap and a hamster wheel that will run you to death. The writer Rebecca Solnit puts it well: 'So many of us believe in perfection, which ruins everything else, because the perfect is not only the enemy of the good; it's also the enemy of the realistic, the possible, and the fun . . .' The evilest trick about perfectionism, though, is that it disguises itself as a virtue."

Elizabeth Gilbert

JANUARY 28

"Writing before dawn began as a necessity—I had small children when I first began to write and I needed to use the time before they said, Mama—and that was always around five in the morning."

Toni Morrison

JANUARY 29

"Many distinguished professionals have been part-time writers—they have pursued their writing careers while holding down full-time jobs. The most successful of them seem to do it by organizing every available scrap of time: they write on commuter trains, they write in the morning before breakfast, they write when they have a few minutes free during the day."

Damon Knight

JANUARY 30

"Always carry a notebook. And I mean always. The short-term memory only retains information for three minutes; unless it is committed to paper you can lose an idea forever."

Will Self

JANUARY 31

"Just write every day of your life. Read intensely. Then see what happens. Most of my friends who are put on that diet have very pleasant careers."

Ray Bradbury

February

FEBRUARY 1

"If you have a job that does not completely occupy your mind, you may be able to plan out the day's writing at work, and so be ready to start the moment you sit down at the keyboard. Being a little frustrated about keyboard time may not be a bad thing."

Damon Knight

FEBRUARY 2

"If you have any young friends who aspire to become writers, the second greatest favor you can do them is to present them with copies of *The Elements of Style*. The first greatest, of course, is to shoot them now, while they're happy."

Dorothy Parker

FEBRUARY 3

"If you want to write for children, you have to remember—vividly—what it felt like to be ten years old. Before you grew busy and knowing. What were your fears then? What were your ambitions and losses? Above all, think back to your thirst for adventure and your capacity for wonder, because that's where the boldest storytelling comes from—the adult who still remembers how to think like a child."

Abi Elphinstone

FEBRUARY 4

"Writing a book is a horrible, exhausting struggle, like a long bout with some painful illness. One would never undertake such a thing if one were not driven on by some demon whom one can neither resist nor understand."

George Orwell

FEBRUARY 5

"The historian records, but the novelist creates."

E.M. Forster

FEBRUARY 6

"Substitute 'damn' every time you're inclined to write 'very;' your editor will delete it and the writing will be just as it should be."

Mark Twain

FEBRUARY 7

"Resilience and humility. These go hand-in-hand, because rejection and criticism are part of a writer's life. Informed feedback is useful and necessary, but some of the greatest writers were rejected multiple times. Being able to pick yourself up and keep going is invaluable if you're to survive your work being publicly assessed. The harshest critic is often inside your own head. These days I can usually calm that particular critic down by feeding her a biscuit and giving her a break, although in the early days I sometimes had to take a week off before she'd take a more kindly view of the work in progress. Part of the reason there were seven years between having the idea for *Philosopher's Stone* and getting it published, was that I kept putting the manuscript away for months at a time, convinced it was rubbish."

J. K. Rowling

FEBRUARY 8

"There is no greater agony than bearing an untold story inside you."

Maya Angelou

FEBRUARY 9

"Any writer worth his salt writes to please himself . . . It's a self-exploratory operation that is endless. An exorcism of not necessarily his demon, but of his divine discontent."

Harper Lee

FEBRUARY 10

"There is nothing to writing. All you do is sit down at a typewriter and bleed."

Ernest Hemingway

FEBRUARY 11

"Lock up your libraries if you like; but there is no gate, no lock, no bolt that you can set upon the freedom of my mind."

Virginia Woolf

FEBRUARY 12

"If there's a book that you want to read, but it hasn't been written yet, then you must write it."

Toni Morrison

FEBRUARY 13

"To me, the greatest pleasure of writing is not what it's about, but the inner music that words make."

Truman Capote

FEBRUARY 14

"The most important aim of any of the fine arts is to get a purely emotional response from the beholder."

Walt Disney

FEBRUARY 15

"There is no such thing as a moral or an immoral book. Books are well written, or badly written. That is all."

Oscar Wilde

FEBRUARY 16

"We write to taste life twice, in the moment and in retrospect."

Anais Nin

FEBRUARY 17

"I write differently from what I speak, I speak differently from what I think, I think differently from the way I ought to think, and so it all proceeds into deepest darkness."

Franz Kafka

FEBRUARY 18

"No tears in the writer, no tears in the reader. No surprise in the writer, no surprise in the reader."

Robert Frost

FEBRUARY 19

"Read, read, read. Read everything—trash, classics, good and bad, and see how they do it. Just like a carpenter who works as an apprentice and studies the master. Read! You'll absorb it. Then write. If it's good, you'll find out. If it's not, throw it out of the window."

William Faulkner

FEBRUARY 20

"Working for the wrong motives poisons our creativity and warps our ideas of success and failure."

Ray Bradbury

FEBRUARY 21

"If it is your destiny to be this laborer called a writer, you know you have to go to work every day. But you also know that you're not going to get it every day. You have to be prepared but you really don't command the enterprise."

Leonard Cohen

FEBRUARY 22

"I have nothing else to tell; unless, indeed, I were to confess that no one can ever believe this narrative, in the reading, more than I have believed it in the writing."

Charles Dickens

FEBRUARY 23

"Tomorrow may be hell, but today was a good writing day, and on the good writing days nothing else matters."

Neil Gaiman

FEBRUARY 24

"If you want to be a writer, you must do two things above all others: read a lot and write a lot."

Stephen King

FEBRUARY 25

"And as imagination bodies forth the forms of things unknown, the poet's pen turns them to shapes, and gives to airy nothings a local habitation and a name."

William Shakespeare

FEBRUARY 26

"You can make anything by writing."

C.S. Lewis

FEBRUARY 27

"Ideas are like rabbits. You get a couple and learn how to handle them, and pretty soon you have a dozen."

John Steinbeck

FEBRUARY 28

"The purpose of a writer is to keep civilization from destroying itself."

Albert Camus

FEBRUARY 29

"On the elusive gift of blending austerity of craft with elasticity of allure."

Joyce Carol Oates

March

MARCH 1

"Cut out all these exclamation points. An exclamation point is like laughing at your own joke."

F. Scott Fitzgerald

MARCH 2

"You can't wait for inspiration. You have to go after it with a club."

Jack London

MARCH 3

"To produce a mighty book, you must choose a mighty theme. No great and enduring volume can ever be written on the flea, though many there be that have tried it."

Herman Melville

MARCH 4

"Creativity is merely a plus name for regular activity. Any activity becomes creative when the doer cares about doing it right, or better."

John Updike

MARCH 5

"Every great or even every very good writer makes the world over according to his own specifications. It's akin to style, what I'm talking about, but it isn't style alone. It is the writer's particular and unmistakable signature on everything he writes. It is his world and no other. This is one of the things that distinguishes one writer from another. Not talent. There's plenty of that around. But a writer who has some special way of looking at things and who gives artistic expression to that way of looking: that writer may be around for a time."

Raymond Carver

MARCH 6

"My task, which I am trying to achieve is, by the power of the written word, to make you hear, to make you feel—it is, before all, to make you see."

Joseph Conrad

MARCH 7

"There is no real ending. It's just the place where you stop the story."

Frank Herbert

MARCH 8

"A good writer possesses not only his own spirit but also the spirit of his friends."

Friedrich Nietzsche

MARCH 9

"There are three rules for writing a novel. Unfortunately, no one knows what they are."

W. Somerset Maugham

MARCH 10

"Easy reading is damn hard writing."

Nathaniel Hawthorne

MARCH 11

"I hate writing, I love having written."

Dorothy Parker

MARCH 12

"A good novel tells us the truth about its hero; but a bad novel tells us the truth about its author."

G.K. Chesterton

MARCH 13

"When I sit down to write, which is the essential moment in my life, I am completely alone. Whenever I write a book, I accumulate a lot of documentation. That background material is the most intimate part of my private life. It's a little embarrassing—like being seen in your underwear. It's like the way magicians never tell others how they make a dove come out of a hat."

Gabriel Garcia Marquez

MARCH 14

"I always do my draft in long hand because even the ink is part of the flow."

Martin Amis

MARCH 15

"When you give up a bit of work don't (unless it is hopelessly bad) throw it away. Put it in a drawer. It may come in useful later. Much of my best work, or what I think my best, is the re-writing of things begun and abandoned years earlier."

C. S. Lewis

MARCH 16

"The test of one's decency is how much of a fight one can put up after one has stopped caring, and after one has found out that one can never please the people they wanted to please."

Willa Cather

MARCH 17

"Writing is turning one's worst moments into money."

J.P. Donleavy

MARCH 18

"Words have no power to impress the mind without the exquisite horror of their reality."

Edgar Allen Poe

MARCH 19

"I don't need an alarm clock. My ideas wake me."

Ray Bradbury

MARCH 20

"Literature was not born the day when a boy crying "wolf, wolf" came running out of the Neanderthal valley with a big gray wolf at his heels; literature was born on the day when a boy came crying "wolf, wolf" and there was no wolf behind him."

Vladimir Nabokov

MARCH 21

"Unless a writer is extremely old when he dies, in which case he has probably become a neglected institution, his death must always be seen as untimely. This is because a real writer is always shifting and changing and searching. The world has many labels for him, of which the most treacherous is the label of Success."

James Baldwin

MARCH 22

"If the artist does not fling himself, without reflecting, into his work, as Curtis flung himself into the yawning gulf, as the soldier flings himself into the enemy's trenches, and if, once in this crater, he does not work like a miner on whom the walls of his gallery have fallen in; if he contemplates difficulties instead of overcoming them one by one . . . he is simply looking on at the suicide of his own talent."

Honore de Balzac

MARCH 23

"Science fiction writers, I am sorry to say, really do not know anything. We can't talk about science, because our knowledge of it is limited and unofficial, and usually our fiction is dreadful."

Philip K. Dick

MARCH 24

"My belief of book writing is much the same as my belief as to shoemaking. The man who will work the hardest at it, and will work with the most honest purpose, will work the best."

Anthony Trollope

MARCH 25

"And by the way, everything in life is writable about if you have the outgoing guts to do it, and the imagination to improvise. The worst enemy to creativity is self-doubt."

Sylvia Plath

MARCH 26

"Read a thousand books, and your words will flow like a river."

Lisa See

MARCH 27

"The first draft is just you telling yourself the story."

Terry Pratchett

MARCH 28

"You don't start out writing good stuff. You start our writing crap and thinking it's really good stuff, and then gradually you get better at it. That's why I say one of the most valuable traits is persistence."

Octavia E. Butler

MARCH 29

"You can always edit a bad page. You can't edit a blank page."

Jodi Picoult

MARCH 30

"Start writing, no matter what. The water does not flow until the faucet is turned on."

Louis L'Amour

MARCH 31

"Every secret of a writer's soul, every experience of his life, every quality of his mind, is written large in his works."

Virginia Woolf

April

APRIL 1

"Don't tell me the moon is shining; show me the glint of light on broken glass."

Anton Chekhov

APRIL 2

"When your story is ready for rewrite, cut it to the bone. Get rid of every ounce of excess fat. This is going to hurt . . . . "

Stephen King

APRIL 3

"Everybody walks past a thousand story ideas every day. The good writers are the ones who see five or six of them. Most people don't see any.

Orson Scott

APRIL 4

"For a person whose sole burning ambition is to write—like myself—college is useless beyond the sophomore year."

William Styron

APRIL 5

"Don't bend; don't water it down; don't try to make it logical; don't edit your own soul according to the fashion. Rather, follow your intense obsessions mercilessly."

Franz Kafka

APRIL 6

"If the book is true, it will find an audience that is meant to read it."

Wally Lamb

APRIL 7

"You need courage. Fear of failure is the saddest reason on earth not to do what you were meant to do. I finally found the courage to start submitting my first book to agents and publishers at a time when I felt a conspicuous failure. Only then did I decide that I was going to try this one thing that I always suspected I could do, and, if it didn't work out, well, I'd faced worse and survived. Ultimately, wouldn't you rather be the person who actually finished the project you're dreaming about, rather than the one who talks about 'always having wanted to'?"

J. K. Rowling

APRIL 8

"I can shake off everything as I write; my sorrows disappear, my courage is reborn."

Anne Frank

APRIL 9

"A professional writer is an amateur who didn't quit."

Richard Bach

APRIL 10

"People say, "What advice do you have for people who want to be writers? I say, they don't really need advice, they know they want to be writers, and they're gonna do it. Those people who know that they really want to do this and are cut out for it, they know it."

R.L. Stine

APRIL 11

"I believe myself that a good writer doesn't really need to be told anything except to keep at it."

Chinua Achbe

APRIL 12

"Style is to forget all styles."

Jules Renard

APRIL 13

"Beware of advice—even this."

Carl Sandburg

APRIL 14

"Writers will do anything to avoid writing, and do it all in the name of writing."

Matthew Kelly

APRIL 15

"I don't believe in being serious about anything. I think life is too serious to be taken seriously."

Ray Bradbury

APRIL 16

"There is only one plot—things are not what they seem."

Jim Thompson

APRIL 17

"Writers live twice. They go along with their regular life, just like anyone in the grocery store, crossing the street, getting dressed for work in the morning. But there's another part of them that they have been training. The one that lives every second at a time. That sits down and sees their life again and goes over it. Looks at the texture and details."

Natalie Goldberg

APRIL 18

"We are all apprentices in a craft where no one ever becomes a master."

Ernest Hemingway

APRIL 19

"The freelance writer is a man who is paid per piece or per word or perhaps."

Robert Benchley

APRIL 20

"You do not have to explain every single drop of water contained in a rain barrel. You have to explain one drop—H2O. The reader will get it."

George Singleton

APRIL 21

"When I say work I only mean writing. Everything else is just odd jobs."

Margaret Laurence

APRIL 22

"The difference between the almost right word and the right word is . . . the difference between the lightning bug and the lightning."

Mark Twain

APRIL 23

"Remember: Plot is no more than footprints left in the snow after your characters have run by on their way to incredible destinations."

Ray Bradbury

APRIL 24

"Do not hoard what seems good for a later place in the book, or for another book; give it, give it all, give it now."

Annie Dillard

APRIL 25

"A book is simply the container of an idea—like a bottle; what is inside the book is what matters."

Angela Carter

APRIL 26

"I almost always urge people to write in the first person. . . . Writing is an act of ego and you might as well admit it."

William Zinsser

APRIL 27

"When writing a novel a writer should create living people; people, not characters. A character is a caricature."

Ernest Hemingway

APRIL 28

"Write while the heat is in you. ... The writer who postpones the recording of his thoughts uses an iron which has cooled to burn a hole with."

Henry David Thoreau

APRIL 29

"You don't actually have to write anything until you've thought it out. This is an enormous relief, and you can sit there searching for the point at which the story becomes a toboggan and starts to slide."

Marie de Nervaud, WD

APRIL 30

"Whether a character in your novel is full of choler, bile, phlegm, blood or plain old buffalo chips, the fire of life is in there, too, as long as that character lives."

James Alexander Thorn

May

MAY 1

"Anyone who is going to be a writer knows enough at fifteen to write several novels."

May Sarton

MAY 2

"We find what we are looking for. If we are looking for life and love and openness and growth, we are likely to find them. If we are looking for witchcraft and evil, we'll likely find them, and we may get taken over by them."

Madeleine L'Engle

MAY 3

"The most beautiful things are those that madness prompts and reason writes."

Andre Gide

MAY 4

"Literature is strewn with the wreckage of men who have minded beyond reason the opinions of others."

Virginia Woolf

MAY 5

"The writer cannot make the seas of distraction stand still, but he [or she] can at times come between the madly distracted and the distractions."

Saul Bellow

MAY 6

"It's none of their business that you have to learn to write. Let them think you were born that way."

Ernest Hemingway

MAY 7

"Imagine the book you would want to read and then go write it."

Whit Burnett

MAY 8

"Rhythm is one of the most powerful of pleasures, and when we feel a pleasurable rhythm we hope it will continue. When it does, it grows sweeter."

Mary Oliver

MAY 9

"Keep a small can of WD-40 on your desk—away from any open flames—to remind yourself that if you don't write daily, you will get rusty."

George Singleton

MAY 10

"I would advise anyone who aspires to a writing career that before developing his talent he would be wise to develop a thick hide."

Harper Lee

MAY 11

"I think the deeper you go into questions, the deeper or more interesting the questions get. And I think that's the job of art."

Andre Dubus III

MAY 12

"Geniuses can be scintillating and geniuses can be somber, but it's that inescapable sorrowful depth that shines through—originality."

Jack Kerouac

MAY 13

"People say, 'What advice do you have for people who want to be writers?' I say, they don't really need advice, they know they want to be writers, and they're gonna do it. Those people who know that they really want to do this and are cut out for it, they know it."

R.L. Stine

MAY 14

"Truth that is naked is the most beautiful, and the simpler its expression the deeper is the impression it makes."

Schopenhauer

MAY 15

"There is something in us, as storytellers and as listeners to stories, that demands the redemptive act, that demands that what falls at least be offered the chance to be restored."

Flannery O'Connor

MAY 16

"Let the world burn through you. Throw the prism light, white hot, on paper."

Ray Bradbury

MAY 17

"Writers serve as the memory of a people. They chew over our public past."

Annie Dillard

MAY 18

"I do not over-intellectualize the production process. I try to keep it simple: Tell the damned story."

Tom Clancy

MAY 19

"The writing of a novel is taking life as it already exists, not to report it but to make an object, toward the end that the finished work might contain this life inside it and offer it to the reader. The essence will not be, of course, the same thing as the raw material; it is not even of the same family of things. The novel is something that never was before and will not be again."

Eudora Welty

MAY 20

"One thing that helps is to give myself permission to write badly. I tell myself that I'm going to do my five or ten pages no matter what, and that I can always tear them up the following morning if I want."

Lawrence Block

MAY 21

"Don't expect the puppets of your mind to become the people of your story. If they are not realities in your own mind, there is no mysterious alchemy in ink and paper that will turn wooden figures into flesh and blood."

Leslie Gordon Barnard

MAY 22

"If you tell the reader that Bull Beezley is a brutal-faced, loose-lipped bully, with snake's blood in his veins, the reader's reaction may be, 'Oh, yeah!' But if you show the reader Bull Beezley raking the bloodied flanks of his weary, sweat-encrusted pony, and flogging the tottering, red-eyed animal with a quirt, or have him booting in the protruding ribs of a starved mongrel and, boy, the reader believes!"

Fred East

MAY 23

"Plot is people. Human emotions and desires founded on the realities of life, working at cross purposes, getting hotter and fiercer as they strike against each other until finally there's an explosion—that's Plot."

Leigh Brackett

MAY 24

"The only moral that is of any value is that which arises inevitably from the whole cast of the author's mind."

C.S. Lewis

MAY 25

"Style ought to prove that one believes in an idea; not only that one thinks it but also feels it."

Nietzsche

MAY 26

"Genius gives birth, talent delivers. What Rembrandt or Van Gogh saw in the night can never be seen again. Born writers of the future are amazed already at what they're seeing now, what we'll all see in time for the first time, and then see imitated many times by made writers."

Jack Kerouac

MAY 27

"Long patience and application saturated with your heart's blood—you will either write or you will not—and the only way to find out whether you will or not is to try."

Jim Tully

MAY 28

"All stories have to at least try to explain some small portion of the meaning of life. You can do that in 20 minutes, and 15 inches. I still remember a piece that the great Barry Bearak did in The Miami Herald some 30 years ago. It was a nothing story, really: Some high school kid was leading a campaign to ban books he found offensive from the school library. Bearak didn't even have an interview with the kid, who was ducking him. The story was short, mostly about the issue. But Bearak had a fact that he withheld until the kicker. The fact put the whole story, subtly, in complete perspective. The kicker noted the true, wonderful fact that the kid was not in school that day because 'his ulcer was acting up.' Meaning of life in 15 inches."

Gene Weingarten

MAY 29

"Making people believe the unbelievable is no trick; it's work. . . . Belief and reader absorption come in the details: An overturned tricycle in the gutter of an abandoned neighborhood can stand for everything."

Stephen King

MAY 30

"If a nation loses its storytellers, it loses its childhood."

Peter Handke

MAY 31

"To defend what you've written is a sign that you are alive."

William Zinsser

June

JUNE 1

"If I had not existed, someone else would have written me, Hemingway, Dostoyevsky, all of us."

William Faulkner

JUNE 2

"For a writer, nothing is so healing as the realization that he has come upon the right word."

Catherine Drinker Bowen

JUNE 3

"Each writer is born with a repertory company in his head. Shakespeare has perhaps twenty players. . . . I have ten or so, and that's a lot. As you get older, you become more skillful at casting them."

Gore Vidal

JUNE 4

"We're past the age of heroes and hero kings. ... Most of our lives are basically mundane and dull, and it's up to the writer to find ways to make them interesting."

John Updike

JUNE 5

"The greatest part of a writer's time is spent in reading, in order to write; a man will turn over half a library to make one book."

Samuel Johnson

JUNE 6

"If it sounds like writing, I rewrite it. Or, if proper usage gets in the way, it may have to go. I can't allow what we learned in English composition to disrupt the sound and rhythm of the narrative."

Elmore Leonard

JUNE 7

"Write. Rewrite. When not writing or rewriting, read. I know of no shortcuts."

Larry L. King

JUNE 8

"Know your literary tradition, savor it, steal from it, but when you sit down to write, forget about worshiping greatness and fetishizing masterpieces."

Allegra Goodman

JUNE 9

"I'm out there to clean the plate. Once they've read what I've written on a subject, I want them to think, 'That's it!' I think the highest aspiration people in our trade can have is that once they've written a story, nobody will ever try it again."

Richard Ben Cramer

JUNE 10

"There are no laws for the novel. There never have been, nor can there ever be."

Doris Lessing

JUNE 11

"Style means the right word. The rest matters little."

Jules Renard

JUNE 12

"It ain't whatcha write, it's the way atcha write it."

Jack Kerouac

JUNE 13

"Not a wasted word. This has been a main point to my literary thinking all my life."

Hunter S. Thompson

JUNE 14

"When I sit down to write a book, I do not say to myself, 'I am going to produce a work of art.' I write it because there is some lie that I want to expose, some fact to which I want to draw attention, and my initial concern is to get a hearing."

George Orwell

JUNE 15

"It's the most satisfying occupation man has discovered yet, because you never can quite do it as well as you want to, so there's always something to wake up tomorrow morning to do."

William Faulkner

JUNE 16

"All readers come to fiction as willing accomplices to your lies. Such is the basic goodwill contract made the moment we pick up a work of fiction."

Steve Almond

JUNE 17

"The road to hell is paved with adverbs."

Stephen King

JUNE 18

"Who wants to become a writer? And why? Because it's the answer to everything. . . . It's the streaming reason for living. To note, to pin down, to build up, to create, to be astonished at nothing, to cherish the oddities, to let nothing go down the drain, to make something, to make a great flower out of life, even if it's a cactus."

Enid Bagnold

JUNE 19

"You have to write the book that wants to be written. And if the book will be too difficult for grown-ups, then you write it for children."

Madeleine L'Engle

JUNE 20

"We write to taste life twice, in the moment and in retrospect."

Anaïs Nin

JUNE 21

"If you don't have time to read, you don't have the time (or the tools) to write. Simple as that."

Stephen King

JUNE 22

"The fun of reading as 'an exchange between consciousnesses, a way for human beings to talk to each other about stuff we can't normally talk about.'"

David Foster Wallace

JUNE 23

"One day I will find the right words, and they will be simple."

Jack Kerouac

JUNE 24

"Either write something worth reading or do something worth writing."

Benjamin Franklin

JUNE 25

"You never have to change anything you got up in the middle of the night to write."

Saul Bellow

JUNE 26

"No tears in the writer, no tears in the reader. No surprise in the writer, no surprise in the reader."

Robert Frost

JUNE 27

"There is pleasure and pain in writing. I believe that basically you write for two people; yourself to try to make it absolutely perfect; or if not that then wonderful. Then you write for who you love whether she can read or write or not and whether she is alive or dead . . . Writing is something that you can never do as well as it can be done. It is a perpetual challenge and it is more difficult than anything else that I have ever done—so I do it. And it makes me happy when I do it well . . . I have to write to be happy whether I get paid for it or not. But it is a hell of a disease to be born with. I like to do it. Which is even worse. That makes it from a disease into a vice. Then I want to do it better than anybody has ever done it which makes it into an obsession. An obsession is terrible. Hope you haven't gotten any. That's the only one I've got left.

Ernest Hemmingway

JUNE 28

"You must stay drunk on writing so reality cannot destroy you."

Ray Bradbury

JUNE 29

"Words can be like X-rays if you use them properly—they'll go through anything. You read and you're pierced."

Aldous Huxley

JUNE 30

"How vain it is to sit down to write when you have not stood up to live."

Henry David Thoreau

July

JULY 1

"It's a feeling of happiness that knocks me clean out of adjectives. I think sometimes that the best reason for writing novels is to experience those four and a half hours after you write the final word."

Zadie Smith

JULY 2

"A writer is someone for whom writing is more difficult than it is for other people."

Thomas Mann

JULY 3

"Let me live, love, and say it well in good sentences."

Sylvia Plath

JULY 4

"By using stale metaphors, similes and idioms, you save much mental effort, at the cost of leaving your meaning vague, not only for your reader but for yourself."

George Orwell

JULY 5

"Success consists in felicity of verbal expression, which every so often may result from a quick flash of inspiration but as a rule involves a patient search . . . for the sentence in which every word is unalterable."

Italo Calvino

JULY 6

"I kept always two books in my pocket, one to read, one to write in."

Robert Louis Stevenson

JULY 7

"Take great pains to be clear. Remember that though you start by knowing what you mean, the reader doesn't, and a single ill-chosen word may lead him to a total misunderstanding. In a story it is terribly easy just to forget that you have not told the reader something that he needs to know—the whole picture is so clear in your own mind that you forget that it isn't the same in his."

C.S. Lewis

JULY 8

"A word after a word after a word is power."

Margaret Atwood

JULY 9

"Tears are words that need to be written."

Paulo Coelho

JULY 10

"You should write because you love the shape of stories and sentences and the creation of different words on a page. Writing comes from reading, and reading is the finest teacher of how to write."

Annie Proulx

JULY 11

"All makers must leave room for the acts of the spirit. But they have to work hard and carefully, and wait patiently, to deserve them."

Ursula K. Le Guin

JULY 12

"To survive, you must tell stories."

Umberto Eco

JULY 13

"Always be a poet, even in prose."

Charles Baudelaire

JULY 14

"If my doctor told me I had only six minutes to live, I wouldn't brood. I'd type a little faster."

Isaac Asimov

JULY 15

"If you're going to be a writer you have to be one of the great ones . . . After all, there are better ways to starve to death."

Gabriel García Marquez

JULY 16

"I write to discover what I know."

Flannery O'Connor

JULY 17

"I doubt I would have written a line . . . unless some minor tragedy had sort of twisted my mind out of the normal rut."

Roald Dahl

JULY 18

"A book is made from a tree. It is an assemblage of flat, flexible parts (still called "leaves") imprinted with dark pigmented squiggles. One glance at it and you hear the voice of another person, perhaps someone dead for thousands of years. Across the millennia, the author is speaking, clearly and silently, inside your head, directly to you. Writing is perhaps the greatest of human inventions, binding together people, citizens of distant epochs, who never knew one another. Books break the shackles of time—proof that humans can work magic."

Carl Sagan

JULY 19

"Words do not express thoughts very well. They always become a little different immediately after they are expressed, a little distorted, a little foolish."

Hermann Hesse

JULY 20

"Writing books is the closest men ever come to childbearing."

Norman Mailer

JULY 21

"Find out the reason that commands you to write; see whether it has spread its roots into the very depth of your heart; confess to yourself you would have to die if you were forbidden to write."

Rainer Maria Rilke

JULY 22

"As a writer, you should not judge, you should understand."

Ernest Hemingway

JULY 23

"A good writer possesses not only his own spirit but also the spirit of his friends."

Friedrich Nietzsche

JULY 24

"The most valuable of all talents is that of never using two words when one will do."

Thomas Jefferson

JULY 25

"The sidelong glance is what you depend on."

Robert Frost

JULY 26

"When you have made a thorough and reasonably long effort, to understand a thing, and still feel puzzled by it, stop, you will only hurt yourself by going on."

Lewis Carroll

JULY 27

"It's such a lucky accident, having been born, that we're almost obliged to pay attention."

Mark Strand

JULY 28

"Words are a lens to focus one's mind."

Ayn Rand

JULY 29

"I am irritated by my own writing. I am like a violinist whose ear is true, but whose fingers refuse to reproduce precisely the sound he hears within."

Gustave Flaubert

JULY 30

"Writing is its own reward."

Henry Miller

JULY 31

"A blank piece of paper is God's way of telling us how hard it is to be God."

Sidney Sheldon

August

AUGUST 1

"I went for years not finishing anything. Because, of course, when you finish something you can be judged."

Erica Jong

AUGUST 2

"I love deadlines. I like the whooshing sound they make as they fly by."

Douglas Adams

AUGUST 3

"Half my life is an act of revision."

John Irving

AUGUST 4

" Don't be a writer; be writing. Get it down. Take chances. It may be bad, but it's the only way you can do anything really good."

William Faulkner

AUGUST 5

"The scariest moment is always right before you start."

Stephen King

AUGUST 6

"To pay attention, this is our endless and proper work."

Mary Oliver

AUGUST 7

"If you want to write a good 200 page book, write 400 pages and edit it down to 200 pages. If you want to write a great 200 page book, write 600 pages and edit like your life deopends on it."

Matthew Kelly

AUGUST 8

"Great writers play to their strengths. If you're hilarious, let yourself be funny. If you have an ear for dialogue, keep your characters talking. If you have a sixth sense for plotting and suspense, write a mystery."

Arlaina Tibebsky

AUGUST 9

"We have to support each other in undoing this myth that we are only working when we are literally writing words down. There are plenty of odes to the Butt-In-Chair mindset of writing—I have both received that kind of advice and given it numerous times."

Lily Brooks-Dalton

AUGUST 10

"If it is true that a story's start is visualized as the left-most point on a line plot, then it is also true that a story is a stone fruit—a peach or plum—and its beginning is the pit on which we crack our teeth."

Bill Cheng

AUGUST 11

"If you are fortunate enough to spend time with strangers who will tell you very harmless facts about their lives, very often, you will be allowed to enter their intimate space as they remember their lives."

Min Jin Lee

AUGUST 12

"By writing about your experiences, you transform your memories into tangible monuments. You validate what happened to you from your own perspective, with your own creativity."

Alissa Torres

AUGUST 13

"Six years after solemnly swearing to all who would listen that I would never take another writing workshop again, I flew off to Portland, Oregon last month to take another writing workshop."

Molly Tolsky

AUGUST 14

"I find it remarkably comforting that someone who had recently finished a 1,079 page novel ends up right back where any young student does, trying to work out how to write every day."

Kristopher Jansma

AUGUST 15

"For every one of my books, there's been a 'cut file,' sometimes hundreds of pages long, of stuff that (much as I may have loved it) wrecked the pace of the novel as a whole. When it comes to killing your darlings, there's no such thing as too brutal if you're sacrificing them on the altar of pacing."

Alison Gaylin

AUGUST 16

"For years I took the old creative writing adage of 'show, don't tell' to heart. I'd detail every trip my characters took to the bank, the bar, the bathroom. They were stuck in micro-orbits of the same quotidian actions; I produced bloated scenes that barely moved their stories forward. It took writing—then scrapping—hundreds of pages of writing for me to realize I needed to shake off that conventional wisdom."

Patricia Park

AUGUST 17

"Very often, the most effective humor in writing doesn't come from a clever concept, or a turn of phrase, or a one-liner, or a bit of killer dialogue. Instead, it comes from the manipulation of carefully built structures, from the ways in which you introduce well known patterns, then undermine those patterns with revealing character action."

Mike Scalise

AUGUST 18

"How? For many years—since long before I could call myself a writer—I've sat through the Q&A sections of authors' book readings, impatiently listening to the usual questions—"where do you get your ideas?" and "what are your inspirations?" and "can you support yourself on your writing?"—waiting for some other audience member to ask this most basic question. How do you write?"

Stefan Merrill Block

AUGUST 19

"Obsession is a large part of being human, and therefore a large part of writing about being human. As writers, we are taught to write toward our own obsessions, using them as catalysts and fuel for our stories. But I have recently been considering how to use obsession—whether it's a character's obsession or the writer's—on a smaller level: not only using it to help us to know what to write about, but also how to write."

Molly Prentiss

AUGUST 20

"Just set one day's work in front of the last day's work. That's the way it comes out. And that's the only way it does."

John Steinbeck

AUGUST 21

"If you have an idea for a short story or a novel and want to get started, write a scene that feels urgent, important, and essential. Don't feel you must write a "beginning," unless that beginning has an immediacy that tugs at you. After writing that first compelling moment, write another that feels just as important and essential and then another and another. I call this "writing to the tension."

Andrea Chapin

AUGUST 22

"Consolation for those moments when you can't tell whether you're "the divinest genius or the greatest fool in the world."

Virginia Woolf

AUGUST 23

"Writing is hard for every last one of us . . . Coal mining is harder. Do you think miners stand around all day talking about how hard it is to mine for coal? They do not. They simply dig."

Cheryl Strayed

AUGUST 24

"Time frames our experience in the world, yet time is never stable: it is always moving. This morning, I walked my dog. We were out for an hour and ten minutes. Yet during that time I also traveled to the immediate past (a conversation I'd had with my sister the previous day) and the distant past (a childhood memory) and the future (the errands I needed to run later in the week)."

Laura van den Berg

AUGUST 25

"I love a good suspense story—the type of dark, twisting tale that keeps me on the edge of my seat, turning pages, barely able to wait for what happens next. That's the effect you strive for in writing suspense; that emotional investment in the plot. But achieving it is easier said than done."

Alison Gayliln

AUGUST 26

"Here's a literary puzzle: Inboxes all over the world are filled to virtually bursting, yet editors and agents frequently lament (in private) that rather than facing an embarrassment of riches, they don't see much that excites them. What gives? Are all of those hundreds or thousands of submissions awful?"

Dawn Raffel

AUGUST 27

"As an independent developmental editor who specializes in fiction, I help writers to fine-tune their novels. Sometimes a central character needs a stronger intention to drive the plot. Or one character is rock solid but others feel sketched in. Multiple storylines may obscure the central narrative arc; or the stakes should be raised, to build suspense. I love solving these puzzles . . ."

Judy Sternlight

AUGUST 28

"Of course there is no one way. When it comes to writing, my motto is "whatever gets me to the next page," but page one is often the hardest. It took me years to start my first book. I agonized and procrastinated and brooded and struggled until finally, out of total desperation, I just started writing, first in longhand and then on an old manual typewriter: the discomfort of not-writing had exceeded the discomfort of writing, so I wrote."

David Gordon

AUGUST 29

"I learned a lot about crime fiction writing in an odd place—the theater. While I was completing my MFA in playwriting at Brooklyn College, I wrote for a few small theater groups in Manhattan and had a couple of short plays produced. During this period, I also read plays obsessively, and I believe what I learned from the theater and the craft of playwriting has had a profound effect on my novel writing . . . "

Jason Starr

AUGUST 30

"Perhaps because it's the narrative mode that most resembles our interior as people, first person narration is the natural impulse of many developing writers. My inclination was no different as I wrote my debut novel, which I completed mostly in isolation, unconnected to any community of writers."

Kathleen Alcott

AUGUST 31

"The ability to forgive oneself . . . is the key to making art, and very possibly the key to finding any semblance of happiness in life."

Ann Patchett

September

SEPTEMBER 1

"Students of logic and rhetoric will be familiar with the syllogistic formula: major premise, minor premise, conclusion. All wax melts. Icarus's wings are adhered with wax. Therefore Icarus's wings will melt as he approaches the sun."

Tracy O'Neill

SEPTEMBER 2

"Moments of pure inspiration are glorious, but most of a writer's life is, to adapt the old cliché, about perspiration rather than inspiration. Sometimes you have to write even when the muse isn't cooperating."

J. K. Rowling

SEPTEMBER 3

"I jumped into the heads of the other characters in the scene and rewrote it from each of their points of view."

Patricia Park

SEPTEMBER 4

"At a certain point in their careers, most fiction writers, in their critiques of dialogue, cease to complain, 'But no one would really say that!' Perhaps their credulity has finally been stretched by the weird mechanics of real-world relationships. Perhaps they've reached the reasonable conclusion that they'll never know everyone."

Tracy O'Neill

SEPTEMBER 5

"If we think that our reader is an idiot, we should not use rhetorical figures, but if we use them and feel the need to explain them, we are essentially calling the reader an idiot. In turn, he will . . ."

Umberto Eco

SEPTEMBER 6

"I've been searching for a suitable writing space—a place that fits my mood, that feels sacred and creative and peaceful, that coaxes the words from my fingers—since the day I started calling myself a writer. Having decided to leave the business world to write professionally, the physical space I occupied suddenly seemed important . . ."

Dina Nayeri

SEPTEMBER 7

"For an author's first book, I would suggest adhering to a basic plot structure, then deviating where and if it feels right. For example, a character's life in its entirety, from birth to death, doesn't matter. A novel is about a very specific time in history or in the history of a character."

Simon Van Body

SEPTEMBER 8

"You know the least about your life precisely because, for living in it, you might barely notice it. You are from a place and you believe you know it, but your memories are not just unreliable, they are full of research holes. I returned to this lesson with my first novel, Edinburgh, for example, set partly in my home town, and inspired partly by events from my own life."

Alexander Chee

SEPTEMBER 9

"The best bit of that advice, and one I would take to heart as a novelist, is the idea of keeping your readers off kilter whenever possible. If they know what's coming, there's a good chance they'll put down your book and move on to something else. So how to keep your readers off kilter?"

Duane Swierczynski

SEPTEMBER 10

"I've never been a wake-up-at-five-in-the-morning-and-write-every-day kind of gal. I have nothing but admiration for people with that seat-of-the-pants-to-the-chair discipline, but that's never been me."

Dawn Raffel

SEPTEMBER 11

"Luckily for art, life is difficult, hard to understand, useless, and mysterious."

Grace Paley

SEPTEMBER 12

"Be a good steward of your gifts."

Jane Kenyon

SEPTEMBER 13

"I didn't discover serious graphic novels until my early twenties, and—as much as I enjoy them now—the form is freighted for me with envy and regret. I always wanted to be a writer, but the truth is that, as a kid, I wanted equally to be a visual artist. Graphic novels might have been a natural fit for me, if only my second career as an artist had not died of shame when I was thirteen."

Stefan Merrill Block

SEPTEMBER 14

"You've got the words. They're swirling around in your head all day—all night for the more unfortunate among us. You've probably got an idea about what to do with those words, a story that's been sitting in your head for weeks or even months, and you're sure that whenever you access it, it will come forth, shining and beautiful. You're sure of this at your core or you'd jettison all those words, forget it, take up basket-weaving."

Terese Svoboda

SEPTEMBER 15

"Workshops are like relationships in many respects: they can be healthy or unhealthy, productive or unproductive, a fusing of minds or a battle of egos. A healthy, intimate relationship is one where you feel as much enthusiasm for what your partner brings to the table as for what you yourself bring, right? That's what a good workshop can be."

Patrick Ryan

SEPTEMBER 16

"All creative art is magic, is evocation of the unseen in forms persuasive, enlightening, familiar and surprising, for the edification of mankind."

Joseph Conrad

SEPTEMBER 17

"I've recently finished a novel—truly finished, as in it's departed copyediting and headed for page proofs—and I find myself in a familiar no-man's-land, the space between books that surprises me every time with its overlarge helpings of exhaustion and despair. My book took a lot out of me; given the emptiness I now feel it seems that it took everything out of me, that all I am is a container for what goes into my fiction."

Ann Packer

SEPTEMBER 18

"It's so foolish to live (which is always trouble enough) and not to save your soul. It's so foolish to lose your real pleasures for the supposed pleasures of the chase—or the stock exchange."

Willa Cather

SEPTEMBER 19

"I've been an editor for a very long time—let's say several lifetimes in dog years—and I'll let you in on a secret. Although your workshop colleagues will (ideally) read your entire manuscript carefully, generously, and kindly, an editor will begin making a decision in about a minute."

Dawn Raffel

SEPTEMBER 20

"Until the day I queried my agent, I was a closeted writer. I had this vaguely superstitious and probably self-defeating belief that to admit out loud to what I wanted—even to friends and family—would be the quickest way to doom my best hope. And so I never seriously considered applying to an MFA program, even if I suspected that my early and muddled attempts at a novel would have benefited from some professional guidance."

Stefan Merrill Block

SEPTEMBER 21

"Don't brag. Be nice. Anyone worth his or her salt talent-wise is humble and kind. This is because they understand they've been given a gift and people who have been gifted have special responsibilities and are thankful. Keep writing. Be curious about how different people live. Talk to everyone; doormen, waiters, motorcycle guys, your grandparents. Take time to get to know yourself because the problem with you will be the problem with your writing."

Marie-Helene Bertino

SEPTEMBER 22

"You start by thinking about all the things a novel should do: tell a compelling story, create vivid characters and reveal them in all their particularity, illuminate the human condition in general, reveal ordinary experience with a vividness that enables us to see the familiar world anew, open fresh possibilities for language . . . you can easily spend a whole afternoon just listing the requirements, and you should."

Gabriel Roth

SEPTEMBER 23

"Everyone asks me what it takes to be a writer. Well, not everyone, since in fact most people don't care about us writers. Or at least, they mistake the labors of writing for unemployment. Whenever something has to get done in my building, someone will email me saying: You're at home, you don't work, can you deal with this? I generally say no. Because the secret to being a writer is . . . writing."

Fiona Maazel

SEPTEMBER 24

"I don't plot. I started out as a poet. You don't need plot in poetry, you have the page, all that dramatic white space, the ends of lines and stanza breaks to organize and build suspense. Readers hang on every word in poetry—and every word omitted. What readers hang on in fiction is just as complicated but perhaps the unrevealed tantalizes the fiction reader the most. The unrevealed is plot."

Terese Svoboda

SEPTEMBER 25

"In any art you're allowed to steal anything if you can make it better."

Ernest Hemingway

SEPTEMBER 26

"Someone recently asked me in an interview, 'How do you obliterate that voice inside of you that tells you you're a failure as a writer?' I laughed when I heard the question because most of the writers I know and hang out with, from prize winners to fledgling authors, all seem to battle the same anxiety that we're somehow not good enough."

Caroline Leavitt

SEPTEMBER 27

"Talent is insignificant. I know a lot of talented ruins. Beyond talent lie all the usual words: discipline, love, luck, but most of all, endurance."

Alison Bechdel

SEPTEMBER 28

"Two of the most dangerous sinkholes I fell into as a developing writer were very much part of the creative writing dogma of the time, and continue to cause trouble to this day: find your voice and write what you know."

John Wray

SEPTEMBER 29

"You have to tell your own story simultaneously as you hear and respond to the stories of others."

Elizabeth Alexander

SEPTEMBER 30

"As someone who writes both journalism and fiction, I have often struggled with how to balance research and imagination."

Helen Benedict

October

OCTOBER 1

"Finding our material is one of the most essential parts of our work as writers. It is difficult, first, to find material with heat—dangerous material, where one is exposed morally, one's reputation put in jeopardy; where one acknowledges one's own responsibility in some crime of the heart, and is then willing to write about it. One needs to be reckless, ruthless, and at the same time rigid, coming back obsessively to the same source."

Sheila Kohler

OCTOBER 2

"It's always just me versus me. From the moment I wake up in the morning—pack my son's lunchbox, scramble a couple of eggs, feed the dogs, make the coffee—some part of me is focused on the moment when I'll climb up the stairs to my study and get to work."

Dani Shapiro

OCTOBER 3

See how long you can stay in that space, where both things are true . . . That's a great place to try to be."

George Saunders

OCTOBER 4

"All the fiction I write arises from the same sort of impulse: it's a feeling of discomfort, a kind of unspecified anxiety, a need to uncover something that troubles and disturbs me. I write toward that feeling. I try to explain it to myself in order to disarm it, to rob it of its potency. I don't know how this explanation will happen. I don't know how the disarmament will take place, or what else will happen in the process."

Roxana Robinson

OCTOBER 5

"I am at my best as a writer when I write for myself and I am indifferent to publication."

Matthew Kelly

OCTOBER 6

"Once upon a time I thought I could learn to write like George Eliot or Henry James. I wanted to be able to say things about my characters like, 'Isabel Archer was a young person of many theories; her imagination was remarkably active.' It seemed so grand to float above one's tale, giving the reader an aerial view of human nature and human destiny. I loved all the Big Omniscients—Eliot, James, Tolstoy, Wharton, Austen. They not only told a rip-roaring story but seemed to offer up Wisdom with a capital W."

Pamela Erens

OCTOBER 7

"One of the functions of art is to give people the words to know their own experience . . . Storytelling is a tool for knowing who we are and what we want."

Ursula K. Le Guin

OCTOBER 8

"If you write what you yourself sincerely think and feel and are interested in . . . you will interest other people."

Rachel Carson

OCTOBER 9

"Turn up for work. Discipline allows creative freedom. No discipline equals no freedom."

Jeanette Winterson

OCTOBER 10

"You can only write regularly if you're willing to write badly . . . Accept bad writing as a way of priming the pump, a warm-up exercise that allows you to write well."

Jennifer Egan

OCTOBER 11

"Don't write at first for anyone but yourself."

T.S. Eliot

OCTOBER 12

"I treasure the time right after I wake up."

Garrison Keillor

OCTOBER 13

"Try to understand men. If you understand each other you will be kind to each other. Knowing a man well never leads to hate and nearly always leads to love."

John Steinbeck

OCTOBER 14

"Work can cure almost anything."

Ernest Hemingway

OCTOBER 15

"Greater than scene . . . is situation. Greater than situation is implication. Greater than all of these is a single, entire human being, who will never be confined in any frame."

Eudora Welty

OCTOBER 16

"In the wholeheartedness of concentration, world and self begin to cohere. With that state comes an enlarging: of what may be known, what may be felt, what may be done."

Jane Hirshfield

OCTOBER 17

"I have always believed that the man who begun to live more seriously within begins to live more simply without. In an age of extravagance and waste, I wish I could show to the world how few the real wants of humanity are."

Ernest Hemingway

OCTOBER 18

"Anyone who writes down to children is simply wasting his time. You have to write up, not down."

E.B. White

OCTOBER 19

"Before writers are writers they are readers, living in books, through books, in the lives of others that are also the heads of others, in that act that is so intimate and yet so alone."

Rebecca Solnit

OCTOBER 20

"In both writing and sleeping, we learn to be physically still at the same time we are encouraging our minds to unlock from the humdrum rational thinking of our daytime lives."

Stephen King

OCTOBER 21

"You use a mirror to see your face; you use art to see your soul."

George Bernard Shaw

OCTOBER 22

"When you're trying to create a career as a writer, a little delusional thinking goes a long way."

Michael Lewis

OCTOBER 23

"At its best, the sensation of writing is that of any unmerited grace. It is handed to you, but only if you look for it. You search, you break your heart, your back, your brain, and then—and only then—it is handed to you."

Annie Dillard

OCTOBER 24

"There is a great deal that either has to be given up or be taken away from you if you are going to succeed in writing a body of work."

Susan Sontag

OCTOBER 25

"Almost everything will work again if you unplug it for a few minutes—including you."

Anne Lamott

OCTOBER 26

"Best advice I ever got was from an old friend of mine who said, 'you have to go the way your blood beats. If you don't live the only life you have, you won't live some other life at all.'"

James Baldwin

OCTOBER 27

"I want to have a relationship with the reader."

Italo Calvino

OCTOBER 28

"All bad writers are in love with the epic."

Ernest Hemingway

OCTOBER 29

"You don't have to think very hard to realize that our dread of both relationships and loneliness . . . has to do with angst about death, the recognition that I'm going to die, and die very much alone, and the rest of the world is going to go merrily on without me."

David Foster Wallace

OCTOBER 30

"Show up, show up, show up, and after a while the muse shows up, too."

Isabel Allende

OCTOBER 31

"I think we're creative all day long. We have to have an appointment to have that work out on the page. Because the creative part of us gets tired of waiting, or just gets tired."

Mary Oliver

November

NOVEMBER 1

"The germ of a story is a new and simple element introduced into an existing situation or mood."

Malcolm Cowley

NOVEMBER 2

"Work on one thing at a time until finished."

Henry Miller

NOVEMBER 3

"Finish each day before you begin the next, and interpose a solid wall of sleep between the two. This you cannot do without temperance."

Ralph Waldo Emerson

NOVEMBER 4

"Write to please just one person. If you open a window and make love to the world, so to speak, your story will get pneumonia."

Kurt Vonnegut

NOVEMBER 5

"You have to simply love writing, and you have to remind yourself often that you love it."

Susan Orlean

NOVEMBER 6

"Tell the truth through whichever veil comes to hand—but tell it. Resign yourself to the lifelong sadness that comes from never being satisfied."

Zadie Smith

NOVEMBER 7

"Abandon the idea that you are ever going to finish."

John Steinbeck

NOVEMBER 8

"Nothing any good isn't hard."

F. Scott Fitzgerald

NOVEMBER 9

"Only a person who is congenially self-centered has the effrontery and the stamina to write essays."

E.B. White

NOVEMBER 10

"The blizzard doesn't last forever; it just seems so."

Ray Bradbury

NOVEMBER 11

"With almost every book I've written. my secret target audience is the young therapist."

Irvin D. Yalom

NOVEMBER 12

"The most damning revelation you can make about yourself is that you do not know what is interesting and what is not."

Kurt Vonnegut

NOVEMBER 13

"You must be aware that your reader is at least as bright as you are."

William Maxwell

NOVEMBER 14

"However thoroughly we lose ourselves in the vortex of our invention, we inhabit a corporeal world."

Mary Gordon

NOVEMBER 15

"I don't even want to please the reader, I want to change them."

Jeanette Winterson

NOVEMBER 16

"Understanding is not a piercing of the mystery, but an acceptance of it, a living blissfully with it, in it, through and by it."

Henry Miller

NOVEMBER 17

"Do back exercises. Pain is distracting."

Margaret Atwood

NOVEMBER 18

"Fiction becomes a weird way to countenance yourself and to tell the truth instead of being a way to escape yourself or present yourself in a way you figure you will be maximally likable."

David Foster Wallace

NOVEMBER 19

"A writer loves the dark, loves it, but is always fumbling around in the light."

Joy Williams

NOVEMBER 20

"Had I been blessed with even limited access to my own mind there would have been no reason to write."

Joan Didion

NOVEMBER 21

"The true heart of the world is a book."

D. H. Lawrence

NOVEMBER 22

"Sheer egoism . . . Writers share this characteristic with scientists, artists, politicians, lawyers, soldiers, successful businessmen—in short, with the whole top crust of humanity."

George Orwell

NOVEMBER 23

"Consider the way of the scientists rather than the way of an advertising agent for a new soap."

Ezra Pound

NOVEMBER 24

"Man has always been half-monster, half-dreamer."

Ray Bradbury

NOVEMBER 25

"Art is long and life is short, and success is very far off."

Joseph Conrad

NOVEMBER 26

"A problem with a piece of writing often clarifies itself if you go for a long walk."

Helen Dunmore

NOVEMBER 27

"Writers do not merely reflect and interpret life, they inform and shape life."

E.B. White

NOVEMBER 28

"A book must be an axe fro the frozen sea inside us."

Franz Kafka

NOVEMBER 29

"The test of a writer is whether you want to read him again years after he should by the rules be dated."

Raymond Chandler

NOVEMBER 30

"The more circumspectly you delay writing down an idea, the more maturely developed it will be on surrendering itself."

Walter Benjamin

December

DECEMBER 1

"The world will be saved by beauty."

Fyodor Dostoevsky

DECEMBER 2

"The writer must be four people: 1. The nut, the obsédé. 2. The moron. 3. The stylist. 4. The critic. One supplies the material; Two lets it come out; Three is taste; Four is intelligence. A great writer has all four—but you can still be a good writer with only 1 and 2; they're most important."

Susan Sontag

DECEMBER 3

"You can never know enough about your characters."

W. Somerset Maugham

DECEMBER 4

"Perfection is like chasing the horizon. Keep moving."

Neil Gaiman

DECEMBER 5

"Something is always born of excess: great art was born of great terrors, great loneliness, great inhibitions, instabilities, and it always balances them."

Anaïs Nin

DECEMBER 6

"You have to finish things—that's what you learn from. You learn by finishing things."

Neil Gaiman

DECEMBER 7

"A writer's work is the product of laziness. A writer's work essentially consists of taking his mind off things, of thinking about something else, of daydreaming, of not being in any hurry to go to sleep but to imagine something . . . And then comes the actual writing, and that's his trade. That is, I don't think the two things are incompatible. Besides, I think that when one is writing something that's more or less good, one doesn't feel it to be a chore; one feels it to be a form of amusement. A form of amusement that doesn't exclude the use of intelligence."

Jorge Luis Borges

DECEMBER 8

"To have a specific style is to be poor in speech."

Herbert Spencer

DECEMBER 9

"Worst of all, I fear mediocrity."

Fyodor Dostoeevsky

DECEMBER 10

"Attacking bad books is not only a waste of time, but also bad for the character."

W. H. Auden

DECEMBER 11

"We all experience writers block . . . sometimes when I was starting a new story and I could not get it going, I would . . . stand and look out over the roofs of Paris and think, Do not worry. You have always written before and you will write now. All you have to do is write one true sentence. Write the truest sentence that you know. So finally I would write one true sentence, and then go on from there. It was easy then because there was always one true sentence that I knew or had seen or had heard someone say."

Ernest Hemmingway

DECEMBER 12

"We have such a young culture that there is an opportunity to contribute wonderful new myths to it, which will be accepted."

Kurt Vonnegut

DECEMBER 13

"The qualities of a writer . . . real seriousness in regard to writing being one of the two absolute necessities. The other, unfortunately, is talent . . . The most essential gift for a good writer is a built-in, shockproof, shit detector. This is the writer's radar and all great writers have had it . . . A writer without a sense of justice and of injustice would be better off editing the yearbook of a school for exceptional children than writing novels."

Ernest Hemmingway

DECEMBER 14

"To write a great book you must first become the book."

Anonymous

DECEMBER 15

"No art ever came out of not risking your neck."

Eudora Welty

DECEMBER 16

"I want my stories to move people . . . to feel some kind of reward from the writing."

Alice Munro

DECEMBER 17

"Talented writing makes things happen in the reader's mind—vividly, forcefully—that good writing, which stops with clarity and logic, doesn't."

Samuel Delany

DECEMBER 18

"The only environment the artist needs is whatever peace, whatever solitude, and whatever pleasure he can get at not too high a cost."

William Faulkner

DECEMBER 19

"It is in the movements of emotional crisis that human beings reveal themselves most accurately."

Anaïs Nin

DECEMBER 20

"Each day, we wake slightly altered, and the person we were yesterday is dead. So why, one could say, be afraid of death, when death comes all the time?"

John Updike

DECEMBER 21

"Unless it comes unasked out of your heart and your mind and your mouth and your gut, don't do it."

Charles Bukowski

DECEMBER 22

"The art of integrating the ego and the impulse for empathy in a dynamic call and response."

Mary Gaitskill

DECEMBER 23

"Between the wolf in the tall grass and the wolf in the tall story there is a shimmering go-between. That go-between, that prism, is the art of literature."

Vladimir Nabokov

DECEMBER 24

"Short stories demand a certain awareness of one's own intentions, a certain narrowing of the focus."

Joan Didion

DECEMBER 25

"Instructions for living a life: Pay attention. Be astonished. Tell about it."

Mary Oliver

DECEMBER 26

"A book in a man's brain is better off than a book bound in calf—at any rate it is safer from criticism."

Herman Melville

DECEMBER 27

"The writer's duty is to help man endure by lifting his heart."

William Faulkner

DECEMBER 28

"In a country this large and a language even larger . . . there ought to be a living for somebody who cares and wants to entertain and instruct a reader."

John Updike

DECEMBER 29

"To make your life being a writer, it's an auto-slavery . . . you are both the slave and the task-master."

Susan Sontag

DECEMBER 30

"The cutting of the gem has to be finished before you can see whether it shines."

Leonard Cohen

DECEMBER 31

"It is important to understand that you are not writing a story or a book, or a sentence or a paragraph. You are writing a body of work. Whatever you are writing today is just one small part of that body of work."

Matthew Kelly